1. Grönskär
2. Horssten
3. Björkskär
4. Lilla Nassa
5. Stora Nassa
6. Gillöga
7. Svenska Högarna
8. Kallskär
9. Ängskär
10. Fredlarna
11. Rödlöga
12. Norrpada
13. Lygna
14. Skarv
15. Svenska Stena
16. Röder
17. Söderarm

0 1 2 3 4 5 km

Joan and/ Jimmy
So good/ to see you here
hope you can ...on!

Arthur + Sue

S...

Harmony
of the Stockholm
Skerries

Harmony
of the Stockholm
Skerries

Jeppe Wikström

The First Island

Grönskär

The 18th century lighthouse, now classified as an architectural monument.

◄ *Grönskär marks the boundary between the Baltic and the 24,000 islands that make up the Stockholm archipelago.*

I was fifteen the first time I saw the archipelago. A friend of mine took me out in his little wooden sailing boat and my astonishment was immense. I had, of course, been aware of the islands but had never come within shouting distance. I was entranced. I stood on the foredeck for hours, longing for the open sea, but all I saw was one pine-clad island after the other, endlessly.

I didn't get to the outer archipelago until I got my own little motorboat a couple of years later. There, I saw the islands give way to open sea. I sailed on, blissfully unaware of reefs and shallows, on course for a large lighthouse on the horizon. Once there, fright took over. Even though there was no wind at all, big waves rolled in over the rocks. I had never heard of swells and found it decidedly spooky. Waves were breaking around me and I quickly realised I was in danger. Green and blue waves washed in over rocks and underwater reefs with astounding force. I was terrified. I spun the boat around, managing somehow to fumble my way into safe waters, away from rocks and swell.

It was my first meeting with the open sea.

The sea had scared me. But more, it had captured my heart. I wanted to be there again, in the outer skerries. Only now, I knew this was no game. I realised there were demands attached and prepared for battle.

I learned to run a motorboat, to sail and paddle a kayak. I studied meteorology and navigation at night classes. I devoured books and magazines.

I got lost in fog. I tied knots until my hands were raw. I ran aground and got lost in fog again.

Step by step, I learned to deal with the islands and the sea. I quickly found that there is no such thing as learning everything—at best, you amass experience.

As experience grows, so does love.

After a couple of years, I returned to the lighthouse island; by now, confidently reading a nautical map and using a compass. I had learned that the island was called Grönskär. Once on land, I found that the old, disused lighthouse was unlocked. Heart in mouth, I entered and raced up the stairs to the top.

I stood for what was at least an hour, 34 metres over sea level, gazing at the thousands of rocky skerries to the North and East.

My passion was aroused. And it would lead to marriage.

From the lighthouse, its massive light extinguished in 1961, there is a commanding view of the low, granite islands that make up the archipelago. At night, the glow of Stockholm against the sky is a reminder of the closeness of the city.

What used to be a deep, protected inlet harbouring fishing boats has been shallowed by a continuing rise in the level of the land mass. Relieved of the pressure from Ice Age glaciers, land is slowly returning to its natural level.

Part-time overseer Erik Sundström views the islands from the lighthouse.

Exploring the island or perhaps already anxious for their next landfall? Islands in the outer archipelago are grouped in clusters of a dozen to two hundred, often separated by large expanses of open water. None of the islets out here rises more than 20 metres above sea level.

The Catch

Horssten

The wrong sort of catch. The giant salmon trap is snarled with seaweed.

The sea is utterly flat and completely yellow, reflecting a sinking sun.

"How many nets do we put out?" I ask.

"Not sure. Never count the nets. Count kilometres instead."

The outboard motor putters away, inching the rowboat forward at close to stalling speed. Erik Lindström is on his feet in the middle of the boat, feeding out net while his neighbour, Jan Håkansson, steers. I'm crouching in the bow, trying not to get in the way and amazed at how easy it appears to be to set out nets. One after another, they glide from Erik's hands into the water and in no time he has laid out five or six thousand metres.

Later, we make our way to one of the large salmon traps, a complicated net construction almost 400 metres long, held down by 17 anchors. There has been a strong northerly and Erik wants to check that everything is all right.

It isn't.

There are no salmon in the trap, which is filled instead with tons of seaweed. Erik tries to shake it out but has to give up.

"The whole trap will have to come up," he sighs. "But not today."

Safely back in the cabin, Erik fixes dinner: an obligatory schnapps, potatoes the size of tennis balls and fried flounder. Not long after dinner, Erik and Jan turn in. It's too early for me, so I take a stroll around the island.

Peering into the heather and grass, I see the foundations of several ruined dwellings, a relic of Horssten's heyday, two or three hundred years back.

◀ When fishing was at its peak, about a hundred cabins crowded the island. Today, only a handful remain.

In those days, there were approximately a hundred cabins on the island. The fishing attracted not only people from the Stockholm archipelago but also from Finland. Nobody lived in the outer skerries all year round, mostly because there was no fresh water and no arable land but also because these ostensibly idyllic islets are totally unprotected from the vicious winter

storms that sweep through. During fishing season—summer and autumn—there were often several hundred fishermen camping on the islands.

There are about ten cabins left and Erik is the only remaining professional fisherman. He lives on Harö island, in the inhabited part of the archipelago, but works the waters around Horssten. In summer, he'll often be out a couple of times a week.

Half-past four and Erik's alarm clock shatters our sleep. It is a delicate, early summer morning, filled with the bird calls of the outer archipelago. We sit, listening, with the window of the cabin wide open. But breakfast is not a leisurely affair.

"The nets will have to be drawn up before the gulls snatch the fish," Erik explains.

While taking us to the first net, he describes how gulls swoop to steal fish caught in the skein. More than a few times, he had found seagulls tangled in the nets, up to a couple of metres below the surface.

Pulling up nets is slow work compared to laying them, especially as Erik insists on immediately preparing them in the boat, so they will be ready to be laid again. After ten nets, he has seven whitefish and about a dozen flounder. Suddenly he hisses:

"Keep still!"

He has spied a flock of mergansers. Erik tells me that frightened mergansers tend to dive and can easily get caught in the nets. I can't work out whether his concern is for the birds or the nets but we don't move a muscle until the flock moves on.

It looks like a generous catch. By seven, all the nets have been drawn up and Erik can tot up a day's work: about 50 whitefish, at least as many flounder and a few fat perch. We load the catch into Erik's fishing boat, the *Saga,* and while Jan casts off and steers a course to Harö island, Erik begins gutting the whitefish, his every move closely observed by a cloud of gulls.

For a moment, the world is made up of nothing but seabirds and fish. With Erik mixed in.

Nets are now made of nylon and all boats are powered. Otherwise, fishing by net hasn't changed much over the years. Erik still fishes where his ancestors once did.

▶ *Horssten's attraction was once its rich fishing waters. Today, people come here for simple recreation.*

Playground

Björkskär

Accordion music carries far across the water accompanied by occasional laughter and the agitated, slapping sound made by shoes on a wooden jetty. From far out on the bay, we realise there's a party going on. We lower the sail at the entrance to the bay and can make out Bo behind a piano accordion and Nils

cradling a guitar. About a dozen twirling couples on the broad landing stage. Britt-Marie and Bertil scurry down to help us tie up and before we have time to catch our breath, we're caught up in the swirl with a cold glass of white wine in hand.

In the lull between two tunes, we are suddenly aware of snatches of music coming from the sea. A pair of binoculars is quickly produced and, yes, it's Hans, sailing down on us with flute uncocked. There's general rejoicing as a sort of musical duel breaks out between

Björkskär island's spacious jetties are perfect party settings, whether it's a sit-down dinner or a dance.

landing stage and approaching boat.

When dusk finally cedes to summer night, a sort of pot-luck supper appears. Marshmallows side by side with Swedish hard bread and chubby little sausages cheek by jowl with potato chips. Beer is retrieved from the chilly water under the landing stage.

Next morning, we all sleep through the coastal weather report. Everyone, that is, except Britt-Marie, who notes the wind forecast on a little slate. When everyone is finally up and breakfast is over in each boat, Bertil makes an attempt to loosen us up.

"Get those bodies moving!" he guffaws. "Let's go for a walk and have a nature quiz!" The nature quiz is a Swedish custom reserved for outdoor gatherings when people need to do more than indulge the body in food and drink. The assembled guests or friends stroll around a designated path, pausing to answer questions posted on trees. Points are later awarded for correct answers. The fun is in the inventiveness and, frequently, the wackiness of the questions.

◄ *A Björkskär mid-summer concert. Bo Åkerström on accordion, Hans Lindström on flute and Bertil Öster on harmonica.*

Soon, therefore, a long chain of temporary landlubbers is snaking across the island. Afterwards, there'll be corny prizes.

When there are chores to be done, they're done without the usual reluctance and procrastination. People come to Björkskär island to have a good time and the work that Britt-Marie and Bertil have to do becomes something of a game. They are island overseers, charged with emptying the council's rubbish containers, emptying the dry latrines, dispensing information and advice and helping people whose boats have run aground.

Two pleasures: the accordion and a cigarette.

In "civilian life," Bertil is an electrician and Britt-Marie works at the Council Property Office in the Stockholm suburb of Lidingö. But their careers rank second to their lives on Björkskär. All summer and every weekend for the rest of the year, whatever the skies, they're on the island. Their work goes unpaid by the Lidingö town council, which owns the island, despite the hundreds of hours they spend in general upkeep and helping visitors. They are allowed a petrol ration and the use of a small room in the only proper house on the island. (The two remaining rooms are at the disposal of "fishermen and the shipwrecked.")

In the evening, we share some wine in their cosy quarters. Bertil has just been on an inspection run and counted 62 boats moored in the Norrsundet passage alone. At least twice as many are tied up elsewhere among the islands in the group.

Bertil heaves a sigh, thinking about all the latrines he'll have to empty. He has a choice curse reserved for the klutz who dropped anchor smack on top of a telephone cable on the west side of the island earlier that day. Then there are all those dog-owners who let their mutts run loose, putting island birdlife at risk.

Britt-Marie and Bertil.

"I'll shoot one of them one of these days. An owner, that is!"

Britt-Marie is also in a complaining mood, annoyed over the group that used the communal sauna without contributing their own firewood and without cleaning up afterwards.

To the uninitiated, this sounds like griping.

It's not, it's love. They're playground overseers.

▶ *A perfect summer evening; sunset and wooden boats on south Björkskär.*

A pot-luck party on the jetty. Island regular Åke Hellberg serves ice-cold portions of Sweden's sticky-sweet "punsch" liqueur.

Light is of central importance to Swedes and mid-summer, the lightest day of the year, is regally celebrated with food and song. No midsummer is complete without a maypole, blatantly phallic and thought to be a relic of prehistoric summer solstice festivals.

Almost full in Norrsundet inlet. There's still space but latecomers will have to squeeze in where they can.

▶ *A morning bath on Björkskär; fresh-water is rationed and ablutions are carried out in the sea.*

31

Privacy

Lilla Nassa

Our portside neighbour wakes us with a mighty splash. He then perches, naked, on the wooden ladder from his boat to the water to lather his entire body. Across the inlet, somebody opens a hatch with a bang and squints out at the morning sun. A third person jumps into the water and a fourth makes do, audibly, with a wash in a plastic tub. A half-hour later, almost everyone is busily at breakfast in the cockpit.

Morning chores take time and not until about ten are some crews preparing to depart. Our starboard neighbours seem determined to sail with their spinnaker but appear inexperienced. They talk it over and discuss the pros and cons, fumbling as they pack the big, billowy sail. A little dinghy, with a two-horsepower motor and an enthusiastic seven year-old at the rudder, circles around and around in the narrow inlet.

Towards lunchtime, several boats depart, meeting a couple of new arrivals on their way in. Even though the crews have never laid eyes on each other, it is as though their Swedish reserve has been left behind on dry land and they wave to each other. It feels like the changing of the guard.

Moonlight, and time for the weather forecast. After a day of sunshine, the meteorological office predicts continued mild and changeable winds. The forecast echoes between the cliffs in the narrow natural harbour as we wind up a late dinner in our cockpit. Our starboard neighbours have spread out their sea charts and are discussing further destinations while the portside neighbour is already horizontal and snoring.

A young couple stands on the crown of the island, arms intertwined, enjoying the moon and sea. A harbour neighbour shouts: "I think your kid is awake!"

They wave their thanks and hurry back to their boat.

Mosquitoes feast on our portside neighbour, now snoring deeply. Our sympathies are aroused. Even though we don't know him, we poke him gently with a

boat hook until he wakens. Scratching his face, he thanks us and crawls down to his bunk.

We go up to the cairn at the top of the island and look out over the Lilla Nassa group. There are about 20 boats squeezed in, side by side, in the little inlet and a cat's cradle of lines stretches between the cliffs. As there is no tide in the Baltic, boats can tie up to land. And even though most of the islands in the archipelago are privately owned, you can both tie up and go ashore without trespassing; it's the centuries-old Right of Public Access, which allows anyone access to water, islands and forests as long as you don't damage anything or go too close to private houses. Despite the endless possiblities this offers, there are any number of boats here, packed like sardines into a tiny inlet.

There is a simple explanation: there are not many sheltered inlets in Lilla Nassa and besides, there are advantages in having others close by. If it's mealtime and you find you've forgotten the salt, for example, there'll be someone to borrow from. And kids will almost always find someone to play with. Even parents seem to welcome a little socialising, a friendly chat about the weather report with harbour neighbours will often lead to an invitation to come over for drinks and a few salted pretzel sticks. The scene suggests suburbia, or even a camping site. The difference being that your personal turf is much smaller and not so stoutly defended. There are no high walls to cancel each other out and we do things in full public view that we would, as Swedes, never do otherwise.

I linger at the island top and drink in the light, summer night. Except for the gentle rocking of the young couple's boat, the inlet is totally calm.

Close encounters in the archipelago. The harbour inlets don't always offer solitude.

Almost all light-houses in Swedish waters were built by and belong to the state. The lighthouse on Prästkobben, just off Lilla Nassa, is one of the few erected by fishermen on their own initiative. It has been unused for almost a decade but a local fisherman has purchased a new light fixture and there are plans to re-activate the lighthouse.

There are only a couple of hundred cabins in the outer skerries but tens of thousands of pleasure boats.

If the harbour area gets crowded in high season, there's always retreat to dry land. There are wild raspberries to pick and sheltered corners for reading.

▶ *Some anchor at a distance from land, perhaps to drink in the peace and quiet. Or just to avoid mosquitoes.*

It's like hide-and-seek. I can hear the putt-putt of the gig's engine somewhere in among the skerries. But where? I tighten the sheets, beating up against the wind through a few small skerries towards Nät Shallows.

Trying to follow Gunnar in his blue gig is hopeless – he knows all the short-cuts.

He is nowhere to be seen and there is only the sound of the gig, somewhere. Soon even the sound is gone. It is quiet and I loosen the sheet and hightail down to Stora Bonden. The gig is at the jetty, with Gunnar nonchalantly cleaning nets. How can he have slipped by me? He squints at me and grins: "A little boat lets you be as invisible as you like in the Stora Nassa islands. There's always a way through."

Gunnar Ericsson is a pathfinder. Like an American Indian on the plains, he steals between rocks and islands in his blue gig. He comes from further in towards the mainland where he still has family but spends the warmer half of the year in the Stora Nassa islands. He knows these islands like the back of his own hand. To pay the rent, he fishes and works as an overseer but it's hard to shake the feeling that he comes here just to find new paths of his own. And because life here runs at a decent pace.

The Stora Nassa group is owned by the Nathansson family, who have decided on a seven-knot speed limit in island waters. Gunnar, as part-time overseer, is meant to do the enforcing. But there's no shouting; Gunnar's style is: What's your hurry? It has the desired effect.

I like to think that he enjoys discussing speed. To Gunnar's way of thinking, much of the world is trapped in the fast lane and he sees the archipelago as a haven from all that. His boat is called *Vänta Lite* (Wait Awhile) and he is fond of pointing out that it goes just fast enough to let him see where he is and where he's going. My own motorboat

◀ *Variety and contemplation. The southwestern corner of the Stora Nassa group.*

is far too quick for his taste and I detect the approval in his eyes when he sees me in a sailing boat this time. He helps me tie up and then strides off to brew us some coffee. I don't like coffee but the first time he offered me some I was too shy to refuse. So I manfully drank it down, aided by copious doses of sugar and

milk. That's the way it is. The only place I drink coffee is with Gunnar—nowhere else.

In the afternoon, we take the gig out to pull up a few more nets. It's near midsummer, the archipelago population has swollen by several thousand with pleasure-boat sailors and customers are screaming for fish. Gunnar wants to catch a couple of dozen whitefish and hopefully a few perch and flounder—although he seems to see fishing more as a way of life than a job.

It's been said of the Stora Nassa group that it has as many islands as there are days in the year. More interesting is the topography; the islands rise high, sometimes steeply, out of the water and there are many good mooring spots. This is just the place for the sailor looking for an inlet all to himself. When we are doing the rounds, pulling up nets, we see boats in the most unexpected places. Some have found narrow inlets, jammed between cliffs, and from a distance seem to be stuck to the rockface.

With Gunnar at the helm, I am free to give my full attention to the passing pa-

Gunnar's main customers are the many summer sailors who call in for fresh fish. Flounder and white-fish are his main-stay but he will occasionally have smoked eel on offer.

norama of islands, islets, rocks and coves. Every change in course brings a new vista, equally fragmented into rocks and water. Distances and dimensions multiply under my gaze. I watch a stark, almost denuded landscape transform under inspection to something akin to mountain vegetation. A great number of trees and bushes, somewhat stunted by seasonal winds, find choice spots to flourish in. Crannies between rocks are stuffed with hardy species of undergrowth. If you land, you discover why the rocks are seldom en-

tirely gray; they are covered with intricate patterns formed by bountiful lichens.

When we get back, Gunnar's first thought is to cure the morning's catch. He starts the fire while I prepare the boat for my departure. When I have hoisted my sail, I turn to see Gunnar. He is barefoot and suntanned, with a fish in his hand, apparently sending smoke signals.

Imagine him without the dungarees and fleece jacket, and he could well be the Last of the Mohicans.

Water temperature in the outer archipelago is seldom higher than 18 degrees Celsius. But for those who don't mind goosebumps, Stora Nassa has spectacular bathing places.

◄ *An anchor is not always needed; the islands are often so close to each other that you can tie up between the rocks.*

Seaweed and algae can make negotiating the rocks tricky business.

After-dinner chores. Greater convenience may be found at many other kitchen sinks but none has a better view.

▶ Stora Bonden, the biggest island in the Stora Nassa group, is where all building is concentrated.

53

Home

Gillöga

Wild raspberries picked among the cliff rocks on the southern side of the island. The cake they'll decorate is already in the oven.

If you weren't used to the landscape, you might think it was just a jumble of islands, skerries, rocks, reefs and channels. After a while, a visitor learns to avoid the shallows and underwater rocks, sometimes by swerving abruptly or by hugging the coastline.

Yet it's not navigational skill that gives the feeling of belonging. Only when each and every stone takes on a meaning, when each reef has a purpose and every inlet a function, does the jumble begin to make sense.

There'll be a stone to show you when the water level is higher than normal, another to warn you when it's low. Russian Rock breaks the back of the heaviest seas when the wind is hard from the southeast. And seaweed off Lillskär island tells you which way the current is pulling.

You know you're at home when you begin to notice tiny changes along the waterline. When you find out where the eider ducks have started nesting; when you recognise the sweet smell of the butterfly orchis; when you have begun to anticipate changes in the lichens and can follow the sluggish spread of the wind-bent junipers. When you can pick the berries of secret blackcurrant bushes, to make flavoured schnapps. When you find the rare, wild raspberry canes, where a good year's harvest will yield enough to thickly decorate two handsome cakes. Or when you can tell that the wild chives in one spot will taste better than others.

There's a triumph in getting to know the landscape so well that the smallest change jumps out at you and tells you something; in moving through the same, limited surroundings for long periods, without becoming jaded. This is how you shape your own world.

My first time at Gillöga was in the summer of '83. I was heading for the mainland when my motorboat began taking on water and I knew I needed to head in to land. I chugged slowly up to a landing stage on Västerskär island and when I lifted my gaze after tying up, the island's sudden beauty took my

◄ *From a distance, the rocky islands look barren and desolate. But there is rich growth in the smallest cranny or depression. This is Gillöga Storskär at its most lush, in early summer.*

breath away. Low, rounded rocks in a labyrinth of small channels and bays. Here and there a larger inlet with a scattering of rocks and islets of all shapes and sizes. And shallow—so shallow the seabed shone through all around.

I sat by the cairn on the top of the island

and just stared, entranced, at the low, rounded rocks. Behind me, my boat was slowly sinking and I couldn't have cared less.

In the following years, I made my way to Gillöga as often as I could. But I was unable to feel that sense of belonging—I was still too much the fleeting guest, the visitor. So when an islander rang me to ask if I would like to buy his cabin on one of the Gillöga islands, I was stunned.

Journeying out to move into my cabin, I had misgivings. Would the other cabin owners accept me? I was a Stockholmer, a city boy, and I flashed on horror stories of bitter, festering feuds between neighbours in the outer islands.

My only neighbour on the island was an old archipelago hand, Bertil Nordlund. He was born on another island, in 1908, but spent most of his young years on Gillöga. His great-grandfather was one of three men who bought the entire Gillöga island group in 1855, for 537 crowns. This makes Bertil a fourth-generation Gillöga islander and me a nervous newcomer when I gathered up enough courage to go over to pay my respects.

"Come in," he muttered. "Know how to cure whitefish?"

I shook my head. He told me to follow and we made our way to the smokehouse on the point. He nodded in the direction of a small rock.

"Sit, I'll teach you."

He showed me how to salt whitefish, the correct mix of alder and juniper branches for the fire and how close to pack fish on the grating. He explained at length how to maintain the right temperature us-ing bunches of juniper twigs and different vents in the smokehouse.

My neighbour, Bertil. His cabin was built from crates which brought American cars to Sweden before the Second World War.

I sat for three hours, patiently warming my rock, as Bertil initiated me into the basics of whitefish curing.

I could hardly have felt more welcome.

Several years have gone by. I spend four months of the year out here at Gillöga and it has become far more a home now than the flat I have lived in for fifteen years. There is much I have yet to learn about the islands but Gillöga is now more than my home.

It is my world.

▶ *Harmony and drama all at once— the outer archipelago in a nutshell.*

The winter brings cold and darkness in such abundance that Swedes dedicate the long, balmy summer evenings to pure pleasure. Children and adults, each to their own.

◄ A dance evening on a Gillöga jetty. The partygoers have come from many islands and the soft, warm wind from the sea.

At first, I was delighted to find so many beautiful arctic terns on my landing stage. But when nesting season began, our relations cooled. They began to attack me if I approached; after a week, the attacks would come as soon as I opened the cabin door. I generally get along with neighbours but draw the line when they start pecking at me. I don't care for the holes in my hat.

▶ The single advantage of being attacked is that it gives me unusual proximity to the arctic tern.

Dawn over the little settlement on Gillöga Västerskär.

Many cabins were built in beautiful spots. But practical considerations such as level ground and nearness to a good mooring place were always more important than aesthetical values in the choice of site.

This cabin was moved in the 1860s from another island where it was originally built to be a sauna.

▶ *Sunset and time to put out nets.*

Outpost

Svenska Högarna

The lighthouse lights up at exactly 8.38 pm. Even though I am expecting it, and even though the bulb is only 40 Watts, I am still taken aback. The lantern fills with light and a hundred polished glass prisms gather the beams into a single ray and send it out into the dark.

"In the old days, the whole light structure used to turn. The machinery still works," says Gunnar Hjertstrand, cranking up a machine that turns the large disc in the lantern.

In those days, the lamp was fuelled by kerosene and lighthouse keepers were on duty 24 hours a day to see that it never went out. In heavy fog, a cannon was fired to warn shipping. Today, the light is automated and powered by solar cells and work at Svenska Högarna is different. Even though there's still a 24-hour roster.

Radar surveillance work for the Swedish Navy. Charley the dog keeps Britten company.

The Archipelago Foundation has now taken over the outpost at Svenska Högarna, although overseers Hans and Elisabeth Anderin along with Gunnar and Britten Hjertstrand work for a number of different authorities: among others, the Navy, the Conservation Board, the Maritime Administration and, most of all, the Meteorological Office. Every third hour of the day, whatever the season, they report on weather conditions to the weather office. A quick glance out of the window is not enough: temperature, humidity, wind direction and speed are all part of the job. All require outdoor reading.

"Worst, though, are visibility and cloud height," laughs Britten. "Especially on stormy evenings or winter nights. You have to be out there for several minutes for your eyes to get accustomed to the darkness. Time enough to miss your warm bed!"

Stockholm's outer archipelago is often described as a wilderness and there is something in the description. The weather can be rough, the topography is stark and there is bountiful bird life.

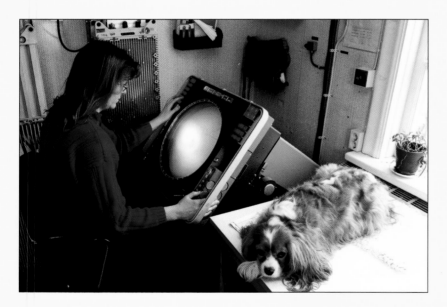

◄ *An aerial view of the main island in the Svenska Högarna, an outpost in the Baltic. Behind the lighthouse, built in 1874, are the staff houses.*

But a better likeness might be a frontier country. For the last five to six centuries, people have been gradually exploring the outer isles. Those who came lived full lives. They fished, hunted, sailed—perhaps even smuggled on the side once in a while. Today, however, the outer islands are empty most of the year.

The outer archipelago is not a wilderness, just thinly populated.

There are few permanent inhabitants in these parts. For visitors to Svenska Högarna, meeting up with some of them is a real joy. The Anderin and Hjertstrand families are the only people who live year-round in this part of the outer archipelago, and the Anderin children, Hanna and Alf, have grown up out here. Svenska Högarna is very much alive—it's never deserted for more than three hours at a time, between weather observations.

A planning session over coffee at Svenska Högarna. From left: Elisabeth, Hans, Britten and Gunnar.

Svenska Högarna is a paradoxical mixture of outpost and ordinary work-place. It's one of the most wind-lashed, isolated island groups in Sweden and yet the families call their homes flats, they have wind-generated electricity and both television and telephone as well as a few lively hens in a little out-house.

People out on Svenska Högarna are constantly checking their watches—they never miss the three-hourly report. They're proud of that.

Both families are gathered in the Hjertstrand kitchen to go through the schedule and plan their work for the coming few months. There's talk, too, of maintenance on the island. Most of the island's houses need re-painting. They will be red, of course, as are most rural houses in Sweden. The colour is attractive against the green of the countryside but the reason is not aesthetic; it's purely practical. The huge copper mines of Sweden that provided much of the basis of the country's trading riches for centuries also provided an extremely useful by-product—a copper-based paint that impregnates and protects wood better than most paints yet developed. In this latitude of climatic extremes, buildings suffer more from the ravages of the elements and every protection is useful.

The major project right now, however, is to find a fireman's pump strong enough to pump water the 250 metres from the sea to the houses in case of fire. There's some conversation about the lighthouse; a few years back, the light-house was listed for demolition because upkeep was thought to be too expensive. Buildings out here suffer greatly at the hands of wind and weather.

A storm of protest forced the Maritime Administration to change its mind and the lighthouse is now smartly painted and a newly formed lighthouse foundation has assumed responsibility for its upkeep. Dismantling a lighthouse is no easy undertaking; it is a symbol of so much that is good that it collects friends easily.

▶ *Moonlight over Svenska Högarna. The name means "Swedish Heights" as the islands can be seen from far out at sea.*

79

The Radamsa in the main inlet at Svenska Högarna shortly after the masts had been put in place.

It began with a southerly storm in February, 1979, and a Russian ship en route from Finland with a deck cargo of timber. Heavy seas soaked the planks on the port side, making them as heavy as lead. Listing to port, the ship sought shelter to the lee of the Svenska Högarna islands.

"We saw them throwing loads of timber overboard, one pile after the other. We almost fell over each other getting our boat into the water from the slipway," says Hans Anderin.

Nobody needed rescuing; the Russians waved us away and instead pointed at the timber, indicating that we were welcome to it. The Anderin and Hjertstrand families needed no second bidding and got to work salvaging as much as they could. After two days, they had beached about 400 high-quality wood planks. Most were thick and long, many over six metres. Wood like that has a host of uses: cabins, landing stages, footbridges and more. Hans, however, had other plans:

"I'm going to build a boat."

That's his profession. Before the family arrived at Svenska Högarna in 1976, Hans had been a boat-builder on Rödlöga island for five years. Those were small boats, though—this was going to be different. This would be the big one.

◄ *The bow of the Sofia Linnéa, a newly built replica of one of the classic barges that plied Stockholm's archipelago in the 19th century.*

Boats are at the centre of everything that goes on in the archipelago: work, fishing, transport and more. Whether it's a tin can powered by a cake mixer or a big cutter, it's a prerequisite for life in the archipelago.

Most new boats are made of fibreglass, aluminium or some other mundane material. But only a boat made of wood will really stir the true sailor's heart.

"We already had a perfectly good fibreglass motorboat that got us where we wanted to go," says Hans. "But I kept dreaming of something else. Wooden boats are different because they have adapted to the elements for more than a thousand years.

That sort of harmony with the sea appeals to me."

Hans made a sketch of a sailing boat that would ride calmly in the heavy seas that can roll in from the Baltic, in through the outer skerries. The boat would be as big as possible without being too difficult for one person to handle.

After a couple of years designing, he began to build his boat down by the inner harbour. Looking at the finished vessel—all of eleven-metres and with two masts—you wonder how it could have been built by one man.

"You don't actually build a boat," says Hans, "you make a lot of small parts that are joined together as you go along. If you don't keep that in mind, building a large boat becomes very hard."

The ribs, the keel, the stem, the deck, the rudder—everything was gradually fitted in place. Since the boat would be in the water all year round, Hans gave the hull a plastic coating—extra protection against ice and general wear.

After five years of sweat and tears, it was finally time for the launch. The boat was quite a way from the water but with block and tackle, Hans managed to propel the seven tonne vessel down to the water. On his own.

"It's best to do things like that alone," he explains. "If anything goes wrong, you don't have to blame anyone else."

The Radamsa with the Anderin family on board in the outer skerries.

The maiden voyage was pure horror-story. It was mid-winter and the entire family was on board. The wind whipped up very quickly and it soon became apparent that the boat was lacking in stability.

"She began to list heavily. The family was screaming, the dog was barking and I was fighting to take the sail down," Hans remembers with a laugh.

Later, three tonnes of ballast in the form of iron and lead turned the *Radamsa* into just what her builder wanted: a beautiful, easily managed and tranquil sea craft—and a match for any kind of weather.

Those Russian sailors might be a bit surprised to see what had become of the timber they threw overboard.

A race using old fashioned post boats over the Sea of Åland has been held every summer since 1974. The race keeps alive the memory of archipelago islanders who carried the mail between the Finnish Åland islands and the Swedish mainland from the Middle Ages until the mid-19th century. It was not uncommon for boats and their crews to be lost at sea. The mail often managed to reach its destination as it was carried in sealed, watertight bags that sooner or later floated ashore. The small, wooden boats use sail if there is enough wind, otherwise the crew rows the 23 nautical mile stretch.

Speed is not the only criterion in the contest; awards are given for well-kept boats and authentic detail.

These spotless boats
are far from being
museum pieces—
they are put to use,
though lovingly
cared for.

▶ No finer sight:
the Vida under sail
in the outmost
skerries.

Solitude

Bogskär

For years, I assumed there was nothing but open sea between the outer skerries and Estonia. Then I discovered a tiny spot on the map—no bigger than a fly dropping—26 nautical miles east of the last islets. It even had a name: Bogskär.

"All right!" I thought. "A secret island! This, I must investigate."

After an hour's journey in a motorboat across open water, we see a dot on the horizon. It could be a ship or a large sailing boat but as we approach we see it's an island. Or two small islands, an islet and several rocks. On one of the islands, there is a lighthouse with several curious seals around it. Otherwise, the rocks are bare.

We anchor at a short distance from the group and row ashore. The main island is full of messages and names scratched in the rock, rusty mooring rings and twisted scrap metal. After a short time, the wind freshens considerably and our dinghy starts bumping against the rocks.

The first visit; Gunnar's father-in-law, Börje Andersson, rows ashore.

We depart quickly. But the brief visit has whetted our appetite.

In the following years, we went back several times but could not always land—the constant swell often made it impossible. But we kept returning. We had discovered that it was closer to Bogskär from our summer islands than it was to the mainland. It may well be in international waters, smack in the middle of the Baltic and half a day's journey from the nearest island but it was still a secret island that no one cared much about. In our hearts, we incorporated Bogskär into the Stockholm archipelago.

◀ *An aerial view of Västra Bogskär island. The lighthouse was destroyed in the First World War and in 1922, the present one was built on top of the original foundations.*

One summer, a powerful high pressure area parked right on top of the Baltic. After a week without a breath of wind, we set off again for Bogskär from Svenska Högarna. The sea is as flat as a pancake and Gunnar Hjertstrand from Svenska Högarna can actually dock his *Sefyr* in a little crack in the rock—the closest thing to a harbour.

"The sea is hardly ever this calm," he says as we tie up alongside the rock.

We carefully study the scrap iron scattered all over. It is all that is left of what was once one of the most famous lighthouses in the Baltic.

Over the years, the Bogskär islands had caused many a shipwreck and the loss of many lives. Finally, the Finnish Pilotage and Lighthouse Administration commissioned a Swedish Senior Lighthouse Engineer, Gustaf von Heidenstam, to build a lighthouse on the westernmost of the two main Bogskär islands.

It was a difficult assignment. The island is low-lying and is completely underwater in a heavy sea. Much of the original structure was washed away in an early winter storm and only after great difficulty was a three-metre high stone foundation put in place. An iron-framed lighthouse was built on it. The lighthouse was inaugurated in 1882 and it was thought to be little less than a miracle that a lighthouse could be built in such an exposed place. Seven years later, however, a severe winter storm struck the island with such ferocity that the lighthouse wall was breached and the three lower storeys were filled with water. The lighthouse keepers fled to the uppermost level, expecting the entire structure to be washed into the sea at any minute. The storm eventually abated but it was six weeks before the men were relieved.

The lighthouse was repaired but never regained its former glory. The lower floors were filled with cement and the keepers had to make do with reduced quarters for months at a time.

Neither could they take long walks. We pace across the island and judge its longest extent to be 40 metres. The tour takes less than a minute. That the staff had time on their hands is testified by the myriad inscriptions in the rock. I find one saying: "1886. John ♡ FH." On every horizon, all there is to see is water.

This is a place of boundless longing.

The rocky inlet looks more like a parking spot than a harbour. The swell makes it almost always impossible to use but on this particular day, we managed to sneak in.

Shelter

Kallskär

There had been a storm warning and since the low pressure trough seemed to be heading straight for us, we needed to find shelter. Looking at the map, we decided to head for Kallskär islands and a well-known inlet there.

We cruise southwards with two reefs in the main. After half an hour, I deliberately change course.

Marika spots an object in the water and yells, "A submarine!"

She points straight ahead at an underwater shape, much like a hull. It is in

An "unidentified submarine" off Kallskär.

surface position with its conning tower silhouetted prominently against an unruly sky. Ola fumbles for a camera and Marika squints into her binoculars. Swedish archipelagoes have been pestered by foreign submarines for two decades and Swedes sailing these waters always keep an eye out for them. It isn't until we're about a hundred metres from the sub that doubt sets in. When we get closer, we see that it is just a rock with a concrete foundation erected on it.

I tell Marika and Ola that they're newly constituted members of the Prackhar Rock club. The first time I saw it, I was convinced I had seen a submarine. And every year, the navy gets calls reporting sightings southeast of Kallskär. If there's one position the navy knows by heart, it's Prackhar Rock.

The inlet we have chosen has a narrow entrance, then widens into a fairly spacious little haven. In the West Indies, it would be called a hurricane hole but

Safely moored in Södervånsviken, a Swedish hurricane hole.

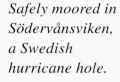

◀ *An aerial view of the northern part of the Kallskär group.*

102

in these latitudes it's simply a good harbour.

Whatever the strength or direction of the wind, there's always a haven here.

The inlet is so narrow that a line can be stretched from one side to the other if there's a risk the anchor may drag. By now, the wind is almost at half-gale and tying up takes us a full hour.

We have barely finished dinner when the storm strikes. Wind strength increases so suddenly that it feels as if someone has kicked the whole length of the boat. The rain pelts down and since there is a leak at the foot of the mast and by the hatch, we spend some time trying to seal the holes with plastic bags and tape. When we tune in to the weather report, we hear that winds measuring 45 miles per hours have been recorded at Svenska Högarna, the closest weather station.

Meditating on the rocks on the southernmost point in the Kallskär group.

The front has passed by morning. The wind is still brisk but it's no longer even a half gale. The sky is almost clear and it's fairly chilly. We take a walk around the island and marvel at some of the installations—someone has built a smokehouse with cement blocks and someone else has bolted a sink to the rock to gut fish in. Underneath the sink is an old washing machine drum for the fish. There's a story to this.

The Kallskär group has about 500 owners. Most of the outer island groups have a system of multiple ownership, a tradition that originated with the very first sale by the Crown, centuries ago. When the early generations died, their children inherited the properties, thereby vastly multiplying the number of owners, and so on down the years.

In the 1950s, property speculators and developers began to exploit the system. They would buy a small share in a property and through newspaper advertisements, sell hundreds of even smaller shares: no matter how small the share, it would still include hunting and fishing rights. The Kallskär group holds the record—there are property owners who own a four-hundred and sixty-four thousandth part of the main island's southern point. Since only a handful of all these people own or have access to a cabin, the rest have had to improvise.

What they've built might not add beauty to the surroundings but is certainly functional.

Diary

Ängskär

Lunchtime music on Hamnkobben; Torsten Sörman's and Nils Rasmusson's accompany the herring and schnapps.

August 1. "Finally—Ängskär! Chimney stacks through the haze after a starboard tack and that wonderful rediscovery feeling. We tie up and landing stage and rocks are quickly covered with our gear. Go on reconnaissance trip and find the house spick and span, windows cleaned and the fireplace ashes gone. But much still to do: putty on the window panes in bad shape and the wooden window frames suffering from exposure. Put out some nets. The outboard motor coughs and wheezes and gets a quick inspection. One spark plug is the wrong sort and too soft. After changing it, the motor is as good as new."

There's a great party going on but I've snuck away to peek into a diary left out in Nils and Birgitta Rasmusson's cabin. It's a huge, two-kilo affair, looking much like an old-fashioned family bible. The first notation is dated August 5, 1976, and copious entries have now filled almost two thirds of the book. In the outer archipelago, there's a diary or logbook in almost every cabin. But nowhere had I seen such an impressive journal as here in Hamnkobben in the Ängskär group. Different owners of the cabin and different collections of guests had left opinions on subjects great and small, and opening the book, you are immediately lost in its wonders.

August 2. "Marvellous weather. Went out for the nets. 8 flounder, 2 whitefish, 1 perch, 6 cod. Gutted fish and un-ravelled net. What a job! Ready by two o'clock. Raced down to the rocks. Hot! Coffee, yoghurt and a book. Wonderful day. Flounder for dinner. Today's conversation: Chinese carpets, fidelity, eating habits, lamps, snoring."

August 3. "Torrential rain at seven a.m. Brilliant sunshine by nine. Some wind in the morning; almost completely calm in the afternoon. Later, dead calm and cloudless! Today's big thing was, unfortunately, lifting up my sun mattress and finding I had crushed a big, fat frog! All three of us there by the water, eyes tightly shut, saying: Eeeeccch! I feel sick! Disgusting! I realised that nothing in the world would make me dispose of the frog and no one else would, either. No way! 'Let's get the Roxells,' I suggested. (Errands bring us into contact with our neighbours, the Roxells, every day.)

◀ *Hamnkobben— which means harbour islet—is the heart of the Ängskär group.*

"'Big trouble,' I shouted when we got there. 'We need help in the worst way! You've got to come over!' They thought somebody had fallen in the water or the house was on fire. 'A frog!' I shouted. 'I crushed a frog! The girls are down by the water and they don't even dare look! I can't bring myself to get rid of it!'

"The crushed frog didn't faze the Roxells one bit. They strolled calmly over and disposed of the corpse. After that, we cured whitefish and perch."

August 5. "Traditional Ängskär party and general meeting held yesterday. Had a tasty smörgåsbord, schnapps, singing and dancing. Weather great—hot and beautiful. Sang, ate and drank. In between, we replaced window putty. Today is hazy but hot—about 25 degrees. What a headache! Can't write much."

Gösta Roxell, neighbour and friend in need.

August 6. "Wind: weak to medium. 22 to 28 degrees inland; in coastal areas, sea breeze and approximately 20 degrees, the weather report promised this morning. 'Weak to medium' wind turned out much more weak than medium when I took out the windsurfer in the afternoon. The only constant was me floating in the freezing water. Got thawed out surprisingly quick with a great boiled cod and a glass of wine. Scraped some more windows and oiled and impregnated the first ones."

August 7. "Our last day began with a clear sky. Clouds gathered after breakfast but the air still nice and warm. Wind directly from the east. The nets we had put out gave 13 fat flounder. After we unravelled the nets, we took a trip around the main island, collecting firewood and casting for pike. Nothing biting. That's when the bad weather hit—hefty winds and rain. Wet through by the time we got home. Stoked up the stove in the sauna and soon had some badly needed warmth in our bones. For dinner, flounder poached in butter with white wine sauce and potatoes. Now, we're lounging on the veranda, well-fed and content."

A discreet cough behind me interrupts my reading. It's Birgitta. She comes over and pats the diary with a tender hand.

"There are nearly 20 years of entries there. If the cabin catches fire, we've got a rescue plan worked out. First, the children and the diary—then we figure out if there's anything else of real value."

*Fishing for stickle-
back from a landing
stage, the prime
gathering place in
the archipelago
islands, where
people work,
gossip, play and
dance.*

*There are buildings
spread over several
islands in the
Ängskär group.
These are cabins in
the southern part.*

The main Ängskär island is a jungle. Thickets of birch and alder make progress difficult. You either keep to the water's edge or travel by boat.

▶ *Swedes long for light and warmth after the cold, dark winter. There is delicious pleasure in taking off all your clothes on a secluded rock and just reading a good book.*

Soft Rock

Fredlarna

Anna caresses the warm, soft rock while Hjalmar soaks up some rays.

◄ *A skiff sails into the harbour inlet on Stora Vånskär, the main island in the Fredlarna group. There are 23 cabins on the island, making it the largest settlement in this part of the Stockholm archipelago.*

By the time we drop anchor, the sun is in serious decline. The air is still cool; spring has not yet ceded to summer. Or, as Swedes have it, dividing the precious summer up into several phases: early summer has not yet ceded to high summer. But when we arrive at the cabins by the protected inlet that forms a natural harbour, we find that the temperature has risen. Hjalmar, who is barefoot, cries out loudly:

"My feet are hot!"

The rocks are wide, smooth and softly curved; they are facing west and have been absorbing sun all day long. Hjalmar strips off and stretches out to tan his pale, winter flesh. He strokes the granite and exclaims:

"It's like warm skin!"

We fall asleep on the rocks and wake only when the sun is low and a motorboat is heard puttering in towards the cabins. We suddenly feel embarrassed and get up to leave the rocks.

We take the dinghy to one of the smaller islands to the south, where the rocks are equally spectacular. Even though the water temperature is no more than 16 degrees Celsius, we've committed ourselves to an evening dip. The warm rocks and the sun lull us into the belief that the water's going to be great. It's not. After a few frozen seconds we drag ourselves up onto dry land, shivering and wide awake.

Two months later, I return to the Fredlarna islands with Björn Ramstedt and his wife, Bojan, from Gräskö, an island close to the mainland. They have a cabin in the Fredlarna group and have invited us to a crayfish dinner. The little red crayfish, *Astacus astacus,* has been a cherished delicacy for Swedes for centuries. In the second half of the 18th century, the authorities banned crayfish fishing before August and a new ritual was born: the Crayfish Première.

As soon as open season is declared, families and friends gather to feast on the boiled crustaceans, always eaten with the fingers. The required drink is

Swedish schnapps.

While Björn and Bojan lay a table in the shelter of their cabin, I sneak away again to the smooth rocks. But the August sky has been overcast and the rocks are now cold and indifferent to the touch.

We eat, sing, toast each other, laugh and fight off the evening chill. Suddenly, Bojan falls silent and points at a young couple, wandering hand in hand along the waterside to the south. Björn and Bojan exchange a smile and a knowing look. They had their own honeymoon here in the Fredlarna islands in 1965. Bojan's sister and her husband did likewise, as did another couple they know.

"It's a good place," sighs Bojan, "There's nowhere better on this earth."

Bojan virtually grew up in the islands.

Her father and three friends built the family's cabin in 1917, when he was 21. Today there are 23 cabins on the main island in the group, making it the largest settlement in the outer archipelago.

"From when I was 12 or 13, I came out here for a week every summer with my sister and a friend of ours. The Fredlarna islands were summer and adventure!"

Suddenly, everybody has islands memories to recount: the time the sauna burned down without anyone noticing; the fantastic sunset at last year's annual crayfish party and that strange incident when somebody had shot through the locks of seven cabins with a shotgun and stolen food and other items.

Many mention the remarkable rocks of the Fredlarna islands. Bojan remembers one episode especially. She sighs:

"My friend Karin Hagfält taught me to dance the *schottis* here. We were out with a couple of guys but all they wanted to do was fish. We had to dance with each other. But we had a ball! I'll never forget those evenings. Nor that smooth, soft rock..."

A longed-for meal but it could just as easily be called a celebration or ceremony. Swedes eagerly await the Crayfish Season of early August, when the crustaceans are eaten with the fingers, to the accompaniment of singing and schnapps drinking.

▶ *An evening dip in seclusion off the rocks almost out in the open sea.*

119

Sandy beaches are rare in the Stockholm archipelago. Fascinatingly, the rocks can be almost as comfortable for the sunbather. The movement of Ice Age glaciers and friction from waves have smoothed them off pleasantly. No one knows how many glaciers were involved nor can anyone guess how many billions of waves have swept over the rocks—all we know is that the bedrock is approximately two billion years old.

The archipelago is made for outdoor living, whether you're based on a boat or in a cabin.

▶ A June evening in the outer skerries. At this latitude, it will be light almost around the clock at this time of year—the sun goes down for no more than four hours.

123

Heavens

Archipelago skies are seldom uninteresting. Here, a cold front is pushing in from the south. The sky will shortly darken and there'll be rain by nightfall.

◀ *A gigantic cloud formation collapses over Grönskär island, affected by cold air coming in from the sea. The cloud had grown to a height of about 10 kilometres during the day.*

Out in the archipelago, there's a lot of talk about the weather. Not the polite small-talk that neighbours are prone to exchange when they meet in the lift, but serious conversations about wind, visibility and water levels. Out here, weather isn't just a topic of conversation—it's a matter of life and death.

There is a certain tendency to boast to outsiders that outer island weather is superior to the mainland kind. The heavy clouds that mean rain for the mainland hardly ever drift out this far. Statistically, the outer islands get only about half as much summer rain as Stockholm, only a couple of dozen kilometres west.

My special kick is to listen to the traffic reports on the radio in summer. There'll be reports of rain and traffic gridlock as I'm lying in the sun on a rock, gossiping with seagulls. Towards the mainland, I can spot a storm front that has stopped halfway between me and Stockholm.

At a distance, rainclouds can look surprisingly handsome.

It's a sizzling hot July day at Gillöga—over 25 degrees in the shade and almost no wind at all. We're curing fish and chatting while we watch the glowing coals. I don't know who saw it first, but suddenly we're both staring towards the northeast. In an otherwise cloudless sky, a white cloud is scudding along at low altitude. Normally, a cloud does not excite general, public interest, not even in a cloudless sky.

This one's different. Firstly, it's not deep but maybe two or three kilometres wide. Secondly, it's travelling against the direction of the wind. And thirdly, it's making a noise—a hissing noise that makes you think of wind in among aspen leaves.

An omen in the sky over Gillöga; the scientific name is Cumolunimbus arcus— an unusual form of shower cloud.

The cloud is moving towards us at a fair lick. It is rolling across the sky. When it gets close, all of Gillöga stops what it's doing and looks up. Nobody says anything; even the birds seem to have fallen silent. It is decidedly spooky and there are goose bumps along my spine.

"An omen in the sky,"someone mutters.

The hissing sound is strong now and the cloud tumbles on until suddenly, we're in its shadow. Somewhere, a dog is baying mournfully. The only other sound is the hissing.

When the cloud passes, the wind suddenly changes and a colder breeze sets in from the north. Gillöga slowly comes back to life, the birds resume their twittering and we go back to prodding the coals.

Somebody goes into my cabin and, after

A shower cloud releases the last of its rain over one of the outer skerries just as the sun sets.

a search, finds the phenomenon listed in a book on meteorology. The cloud type is called *Cumolunimbus arcus* and is an unusual variation on a shower cloud. It forms when two equally dry masses meet and it is, in effect, a tiny cold front.

Everything happens in the sky. Pressure and humidity make the sea beautiful or dangerous; clouds warn of what is about to take place. Which is why islanders often bend their necks. Upwards, towards the heavens.

▶ *Spring is fog season. Fog forms when warm air blowing in from the south is cooled over the sea.*

131

Despite weather predictions and warning signs in the sky, storms can still take you by surprise. Two islanders are trying to save a boat left behind at a landing stage.

A winter storm. Waves have been gathering momentum all across the Baltic and hit the rocks with force. The highest wave recorded in the Baltic was 12.8 metres high.

Thunder and lightning. Thunderstorms are unusual in the outer archipelago; that kind of weather occurs only about six days a year. But when it happens, it can be frightening—the acoustics are especially good out here and thunder sounds really mean as it rolls over the water, resounding between stony cliffs.

▶ *Dead calm in the outer archipelago. Strange phenomena can occur in the sea breeze. Here, the sea breeze is battling with a westerly wind. When the picture was taken, the westerly was at a strength of 20 miles per hour and out at sea, there was an almost equally strong southeasterly. But here, there's not a breath of wind. Only the clouds over the mainland witness to any wind at all in the area.*

The General Store

Rödlöga

It could almost be an idyllic corner of inland countryside. On the steps to the perfect, red-painted, two-storey house sits Eva Fristedt, surrounded by geraniums and other pot plants. She is patting Oliver, the cat. Bumble bees buzz around the currant bushes and there's the sound of a power lawnmower from the other side of Byviken inlet.

The fruits of modern society are seldom for the outer archipelago; out here, there is no electricity, no phones and no mail. Many of the smaller islands even lack a freshwater well.

Rödlöga island, however, is an outpost of civilisation among the skerries. There are a postal service, regular ferries, a telephone booth and, best of all—a general store.

Eva Fristedt runs the store, the living heart of this outer group of islands. The store belongs to a cooperative in which almost all the cabinowners out here are members. There are a hundred or so households in the Rödlöga group, although no one lives year-round any longer.

The store is quite modern. Since there are no electricity mains on the island, the cooperative has installed a little generator providing current for the shop's freezers. Neon lighting shows off what the shop has to offer in the way of meat, vegetables, fruit, candy, saltwater soap, ice cream, breakfast cereal—and eleven different kinds of glass globes for kerosene lamps, the island's principal source of light.

Rödlöga society personalities, Eva Fristedt and Oliver the cat.

Everything has to be brought here by the passenger boat that docks at Rödlöga every day in summer. Every visit is an electrifying event for the island.

The boat brings mail, fresh newspapers and goods. There is often construction material as deck cargo and complete sets of furniture are not unusual.

Most fun of all is to see the people who disembark. If you've been out in the islands for a couple of months, you feel like a native on some distant, South Sea island. You tend to stare open-mouthed at folk when the boat—your only connection with civilisation—arrives. People arriving directly from Stockholm seem like another, vastly more sophisticated, race.

◄ *The jetty at Rödlöga is a border outpost linking civilisation and the wilderness of the skerries. The shop to the right is the pulsing heart of this verdant island group.*

At times like these, the immediate area of the steamboat jetty explodes in activity. Day trippers make a beeline for the little café just outside the general store. Summer islanders collect visiting friends, balancing their bags precariously on

small wheelbarrows; small craft start loading what was off-loaded from the passenger boat.

Eva closes the store while the boat is in, to give her time to place perishable produce in the proper shelves and freezers; the customers wait patiently outside. When everything is shipshape, Eva comes out and announces that purchasing can resume; the store fills with excited customers as well as curious tourists.

"Easy, now!" shouts Eva, laughing. "There's yoghurt at the back of the dairy fridge. There's fresh *entrecôte* and we've got some great Camembert."

An object hanging from the ceiling makes customers crane their necks as they pass. It's a map of the island, with an old key to denote each building in the island group. When the former shopowner died, they found he had kept copies of keys to every house and cabin on the entire island. It has always been something of an artists' haven so the idea came quickly and the map was just as quickly put together.

Each key on the map denotes a cabin or house in the Rödlöga group.

Rödlöga is very much a living island.

There may be no permanent inhabitants left but many of the summer islanders are descendants; they take great care of the islands. There is constant, creative activity: the store was organised and set up, the café was started and now some youngsters have a "kids' cabin" where they can hang out on summer evenings.

For an outsider, getting around the main island is difficult. There's both a maze of paths through something that looks like virgin forest and also an area packed with cabins built almost on top of each other. It's hard to walk anywhere without the feeling that you're trespassing. The Rödlöga islanders have put up small signs to help visitors find their way—and perhaps to avoid having to field questions.

Signs sprout freely on Rödlöga. This one indicates the way to the shop and to the west side of the island. It also carries a snake warning.

You can still get lost.

Just as the general store is about to shut, an older man approaches, puffing, mosquito-stung and sweating. He says he has been lost and that it took an hour for him to get from the west side of the main island to the east, normally a fifteen-minute stroll.

Eva laughs her hearty laugh and comforts him with an ice cream. When he sees the newspapers, fresh from the city, his face splits in a contented grin. Perfect happiness! Clutching ice cream and newspaper, he heads straight for the telephone booth to call home.

▶ *Dawn over the sea off Rödlöga. The spellbinding song of the nightingale complements the magic of the Nordic light.*

145

Rödlöga is something of an artists' island group; no pump remains merely a pump but becomes an exclamation mark. On a wall beside the shop, an old boot is filled daily with fresh flowers.

A rural idyll, far out in the Baltic. A towel has been hung out to dry in the tranquil summer evening and there is the scent of freshly brewed coffee from the cottage at the end of the inlet.

▶ To the lighthouse. Half the day has been spent preparing for the outing and since there is little maritime traffic, the evening picnic promises to be undisturbed.

149

The Rockies

Norrpada

Picnic with accordion on Spegelkobben island.

We clamber over giant blocks of stone and steep rocks to get to the top of the island. Once there, 20 metres up, we sit down, out of breath and speechless from the beauty and drama of the landscape. From here, the entire island group seems to consist of high, steep islands.

"People sometimes fall and get hurt. Mostly scrapes and grazes but there have been a few broken limbs," says Sten.

His family name is Söderlund and he is an overseer, working for the Archipelago Foundation and in charge of several island groups, among them Norrpada. This means he's responsible for everything plus the kitchen sink. He also keeps an eye on inexperienced people let loose in the islands. And he is there with bandages and antiseptic when people take a tumble.

The Norrpada islands are one of the most popular outer archipelago destinations for pleasure boats. In mid-July, there might be up to a hundred boats tied up overnight. And everyone wants to climb the islands.

"It's like we're drawn to that high spot," says Sten. "And not just for the view; there may well be some ancient instinct of self-protection, to always want to see what's around you."

◄ *Storm clouds over Norrpada. The tall islands create a dramatic landscape.*

Suddenly, the sharp sound of a steam whistle echoes among the rocks. It's the *SS Saltsjön*, built in 1925, out on one of its charter trips. There's no regular ferry out here but the few charter boats that venture out are always full.

A voice is heard from the steamer's loudspeaker:

156

"The Norrpada islands are the result of prodigious work by Nature. The bedrock was formed about two billion years ago. Since then, the region has been repeatedly shaken by earthquakes and fault shifts, like those that formed the Alps and fjords and other landmarks. Then came the Ice Age glaciers to smooth out the bumps, rather like sandpaper."

We move to the island where the *Saltsjön* is tying up and help them. Sten is immediately pressed into service as guide and leads a hundred passengers at a trot uphill through the forest. This, too, is a steep island and it takes them some time to get to the top where the view attracts cameras and binoculars like a magnet.

Sten Söderlund empties the telephone box on Gummaskär island.

Sten is a city kid from Stockholm but the pull of the outer skerries was irresistible and he moved out to the archipelago in the early '70s and began working for the Archipelago Foundation. Today, a lot of his working hours are in the outer skerries. It can be a lonesome job. Sometimes he's out in his boat for several days without meeting a single soul.

"But there's the seals. They keep me company. That counts," he says and the elderly women clustered around him smile in delight.

He should be telling them about the Norrpada group; instead, he's feeding them stories of dramatic sea rescues and the migration of seals across the Baltic. Sten likes seals and protects their reserve, like a shepherd of the seas.

When the *Saltsjön* departs, we motor over to Gummaskär island. Sten has to empty the coin box in the little telephone booth. The grey telephone looks like any other but it is powered by solar cells. You pay by putting coins in a little can.

Somebody has put in a large bill but Sten shows little surprise:

"This is either someone calling a lover or it's an emergency call. When they use the phone for important things like that, people feel extra generous."

We motor slowly over to Alkobben, the biggest island in the group, and ascend the peak by the long ridge on the Western side. Across the bay, there are a couple of families having a picnic to accordion music and on one of the other islands we spot two young guys climbing the difficult Northern wall. We content ourselves with watching and sit down on the smooth rocks to enjoy the picnic we've brought along.

I get a sense of belonging to a chosen few—the mountain people of Norrpada.

▶ An aerial view of Norrpada from the north, with Lilla Idskär island in the foreground.

Crow's Nest

Lygna

If I hadn't known, I would have been frightened. The crow comes at me from behind and lands on my head and I feel its claws grip my scalp. I try to ignore the bird and continue snapping pictures. After a minute or so, he gets bored and hops over to the camera on the tripod, contenting himself with viewing his reflection in the lens.

I'm still pretending I don't notice him.

Axel attempts a self-portrait.

But when he begins pecking at the lens, I start shouting and waving my arms. He flies up and circles me, cawing insultingly. Then he dive-bombs my camera case, grabs a roll of film and flies off, dropping the film on a wooden sailing boat along the way. He perches on the masthead and caws again.

It could be laughter.

"Axel!"

Magdalena's stern cry echoes across the inlet and the crow responds immediately, flying over to her and landing on her shoulder.

"What did he take now?" she asks.

"A roll of film," I answer, adding that it doesn't really matter. Magdalena says something to Axel that I can't hear. The amazing thing is, the bird really looks as though he's ashamed of himself. He makes baby-like sounds and tries to hide in Magdalena's hair.

The Lygna islands have an atmosphere of intimacy. The narrow harbour on the main island, with tall cliffs on either side, feels almost like a ballroom. Since these waters are full of shallows and there are few protected inlets, not many pleasure boats venture out here.

There are only three habitable cabins on Lygna and all three are on the main island, Hamnskär, and the owners are all related. The Hallström and Rinaldo families own the island group.

The outer archipelago has always been a male environment. Out here, men have for centuries devoted themselves to masculine pursuits such as hunting, fishing and navigation, without the nuisances of women and children.

On Lygna today, however, a woman provides the continuity. Magdalena is the daughter of a well-known archipelago writer, Sten Rinaldo, who looked after his islands with great love and care. Magdalena and both owner-families have honoured his memory in the same way.

For example, Magdalena counts birds in the old way and is one of the few collectors of eider down, which provides a nice little extra income. I get the occa-

◄ Safe and secure in Hamnskär inlet, with walls of granite holding out the wind.

sional feeling that she might irritate an unprepared he-man, simply because she does most things better than most men can. She's great in a boat; knows the archipelago like the back of her hand and moonlights as a teacher of navigation. She spends more time than most in the islands.

And she's often alone out here.

Besides, she's the only woman I know who keeps tame crows. Axel is her third. He's from Lygna; Magdalena got him from a nest at the end of April one year.

Axel is convinced that Magdalena is his mother and will let no one else scold him. His favourite place in all the world is on her shoulder.

"Tame crows make good company. And every one of them is a real personality. My last one, Kraka, was quiet and obedient—Axel's the inventive, naughty one," says Magdalena, stroking Axel's feathered back.

The effect of the stroking is to make him stop playing ashamed—it had lasted no more than a minute—and he flies off to the mouth of the inlet to chase away a seagull. He then alights on the windowsill of the Hallström cabin where the family is having dinner with a guest. Axel admires his own image in the window for a while and pecks gently at the pane.

The sun is on the wane, though, and soon he flies into Magdalena's cabin to sleep the night. There's a crow's nest of his own in there.

▶ *An early-morning dip. You jump in and get out fast; water temperature is an icy 16 degrees Celsius.*

The archipelago has always attracted writers and artists. August Strindberg lived out here for long periods and set several of his books in the islands. This isolated cabin, built in 1961, belonged to a more recent writer, Sten Rinaldo, with several books on the people of the archipelago and their history to his credit.

Thickets of St. John´s wort on one of the islands. Picked carefully and immersed in schnapps, the flowers turn the liquid pale red. The herb has been used for generations as a cure for epilepsy, stroke and indigestion. Used in schnapps, its properties were also said to help against madness and insomnia.

► Hamnskär´s inner sanctum.

The Outmost Island

Skarv

Alf is used to sleeping out and is already counting sheep. I'm still not drowsy—a moon and a few million stars are keeping me awake as well as the lethargic lapping of the sea.

We're berthed in Alf's pride and joy, *Klenoden* (The Heirloom), which smells wonderfully of tar and wet canvas. *Klenoden* is anchored right in the middle of the furthest seaward island group. Skarv is not the last island group in the archipelago but no other this far from the coast has been built on and regularly used by fishermen.

Klenoden (The Heirloom) on its way to Skarv. Behind the skerries is the open sea.

There's a simple reason: there is a sheltered inlet where a handful of boats can anchor. The entrance is so narrow, however, that only smaller boats can use the shelter. The men who owned the island and who spent a lot of time there built their boats so they could fit in—just. *Klenoden*, built in the 1930s, is one of these tailormade Skarv boats, small enough to enter the harbour inlet yet big enough to tackle the occasionally heavy seas in the area.

It had taken us an hour to reach Skarv over the open water from Svenska Högarna where Alf Anderin lives. On the way, we circle Söderskär island which has one of the largest colonies of razorbills in the outer skerries. I'm not sure why, but old island hands say that you should wave when you spot a passing razorbill. As we see hundreds of them on our trip, we're bobbing up and down in the boat and waving like royalty.

Approaching the narrow opening of the inlet on the main island, Skarv Bodskär, we are momentarily perplexed. Alf has never been here with *Klenoden* before and I have been here only in a kayak. On arrival, we stand with boat hooks at the ready—there are only centimetres to spare on either side. Luckily, *Klenoden* seems to be able to find her own way and she glides in between the cliffs without a touch.

◄ *A tranquil summer night by Skarv island. It is not always so idyllic; in the old days, heavy winds often forced fishermen to pull their boats up on land.*

Once tied up, we undertake an expedition. The Skarv islands are an exciting place, not least because of all the traces of past history. People have been fishing here since the Middle Ages and even though Skarv's Bodskär island is no wider than a hundred metres, there was a settlement here at the end of the last century of about a dozen cabins. The last of them burned down in 1945 but the foundations of many can still be seen and there are inscriptions scratched into the rockface. There are owners' marks, years, other inscriptions of the "Kilroy was here" variety (centuries before Kilroy) and others perhaps done simply to make time pass. Others may have been religiously motivated but whatever the reasons, this is vintage graffiti.

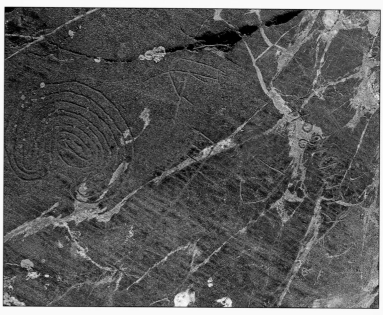

Over the centuries, people have etched names, dates and symbols into the rock on Skarv island. One inscription bears the date 1622; others may be even older.

Corroded iron spikes in their dozens, embedded in the rock, indicate that the little harbour was much in use and also that boats had to be securely tied up when heavy swells came in from the sea. When the sea was at its roughest, boats were hauled up on land to stop them being smashed against the cliffs. There is an inlet from the north which must have given more protection but because the land mass in the Baltic has risen in relation to water level over the years, entry is now possible only by kayak.

To our surprise and pleasure, we discover a large patch of angelica, a bush-like herb, the seeds just dry enough to harvest. Herb-flavoured *aquavit* (schnapps) has a long tradition in Sweden—Swedes are as learned about schnapps as the French are with wine. Over 50 wild herbs, berries and grasses are commonly used for flavouring this strong and noble spirit. Before darkness falls, we have each filled an enamel mug. Back on board *Klenoden*, we cook a fish soup on the old primus and make a few bread and butter sandwiches.

The likelihood of anyone coming by after dark is not great. But Alf hoists a

hurricane lamp on the mast, warning others that we have lines stretched across the inlet. The light spreads a pleasurable glow over the little natural harbour, competing on a friendly basis with the glimmering, silver moonlight.

The bare rock of the island immediately takes on a cosy look.

A mug of angelica, one of a large number of wild herbs used to flavour schnapps.

The northern inlet, once also used as a harbour, is now navigable only by kayak because of the land mass rise after the Ice Age.

Two rock humps in the southwest have fed the imaginations of many generations. This rock formation is called The Bride of Skarv.

We hoist a lantern to warn others that we have lines crossing the entrance to the inlet. The introduction of the kerosene lamp to Sweden in the 1860s changed life in the archipelago. Previously, cabin light was provided mostly by open fires; oil lamps and rags soaked in tallow were widely used but gave off sooty smoke and little light.

▶ Skarv has been called "a splinter in the sea." But for centuries, people have lived here for months at a time.

179

Seal Country

Svenska Stenarna

Seal song wakes me at dawn. Everything is still and the sound of their melancholic, almost wailing song carries far across the flat sea. I lay quiet in my tent on Stora Vitkobben island, listening—delighted but also touched by the melancholy.

I must have fallen asleep, because when I wake again, the sun is high and a soft breeze ripples the water. Suddenly, something glistens in the water. It's a reflection, but of what? I stretch for my binoculars and discover that it is a bottle.

A message carried by the waves.

But can it be? I jump out of my sleeping bag and stride down to the water. It is! A letter in a bottle!

My heart is beating double. All my life I've dreamed of finding a letter in a bottle! I've walked beaches for countless hours hoping for this moment. And here it is!

Peering at the bottle in the water, I can make out some of the writing.

SOS.

Incredible! Maybe it's from a beautiful girl on a desert island, waiting to be rescued. The bottle is still a few metres from land so I run to my kayak and get my paddle. I still can't reach it and on my last attempt, I slip and fall in. I swim two strokes in the cold water and retrieve the bottle.

Wet, I stagger back onto land; but I have the bottle, clutched firmly in my fist. I have sudden misgivings—this is a whisky bottle, and a cheap brand, too. Hardly a drink for a lady. My frozen fingers take a long time opening the bottle and extracting the letter.

It turns out to be two kids from a coastal town further north who just want to say hi. They had thrown the bottle into the water from a nearby island group all of two days earlier. A little disappointed but still feeling something of a thrill from my find, I trek back up to my tent to make breakfast.

◄ *Stora Vitkobben, the largest island in the Svenska Stenarna group. These islands are more dispersed and more isolated than most. Lack of sheltered anchorage anywhere in the group is a problem these visitors have solved by pulling their craft onto the shore.*

An hour later, I am on my way northeast in my kayak. It is usually accepted that Svenska Stenarna are the outmost island group in the Stockholm archipelago but there are a few, very small skerries even further east.

This is seal country. There are lots of low, smooth rocks, perfect for crawling up on to rest and sunbathe. The surrounding open waters give the seals an

excellent view of any approaching threat. Now, the area has been designated a seal reserve, strictly off limits in spring and summer. This is late August, the first week I was allowed in here in my kayak.

The first seals are not slow in approaching to check me out. It's a strange feeling, having them so close. Some are only metres from the kayak, curious but alert. A large male surfaces regularly right behind me, but as soon as I turn around, he dives.

It's not an undivided pleasure having them so close. A male can weigh up to 300 kilos and one little shove and you're in the drink. So I'm tense when a young seal starts shoving at the paddle on the starboard side. I slap the side of the kayak with the paddle, hoping to make them back off. It seems to work.

Within a couple of hours, I see about six hundred seals. It's marvellous, considering that there were at the most 200 in the entire area in the early '80s. Seals are the Baltic's only mammals and are regarded with much affection in Sweden, where the animal is a symbol for threatened fauna. They range over formidable distances; the young male who had been pestering me may well have been pestering somebody else in Finnish coast waters the day before.

I'm heading for Ytterberget. I've been trying to make land here for several years, but because the seas in this area are always heavy, I've never succeeded. It's the same story this time—even though for once it's fairly calm. A heavy swell is rolling in, beating up against the black, slippery rocks. I paddle around the island three times before I can decide on a course of action. I struggle out of my clothes, slip into the water and pull the kayak after me on its rope. I swim ashore, find a few cracks to hold onto, climb up and pull the kayak up.

Finally, landfall on Ytterberget! The tiny skerry is no wider than 20 metres. It has a fairly uninteresting shape and stinks of bird dung. Nonetheless, it is the outmost point in the archipelago, which counts for something.

The seals peer at me with wonder as I stand there, naked, singing to the sky, denying the existence of time.

Heading for Ytterberget, the archipelago´s outmost point.

▶ *Cliffs and horizontal crevasses on the island bring out the monkey in even the most sophisticated sailor.*

It´s almost certainly forbidden but the temptation to climb a sea-mark can be irresistable. The magnificent view stretches halfway to Finland.

The long Swedish dusk settles as seals wail across the waters.

This 12-metre sea-mark is one of thousands of navigation aids, large and small, in a seascape where low, flat islands can easily blend with the horizon. Sea-marks, often built from piles of stones, have been built and used by archipelago folk for centuries.

▶ *Rock, risen from the sea only a few thousand years ago, is topped by a sea-mark from another time in the more recent past.*

Shanties

Röder

The flowers of the St. John's wort herb, a favourite schnapps flavouring, fill the bottle.

◄ *The settlement on Röder Bodskär seen from the north. Lygna island is visible on the horizon and Svenska Högarna can just be glimpsed.*

The cabins have been built as close to each other as possible on a narrow tongue of land. From the north, it's almost as if each cabin wants to be on the lee side of the next.

Together, they hunker down to stave off wind and rain.

Nothing needs protection right now—this is a balmy summer evening; it's almost 30 degrees Celsius and the water is eminently swimmable. There's a full moon beaming security over the Röder Bodskär island.

Someone calls to a neighbouring cabin and a plate is seen being carried out one door and in through another. A few islanders are putting the yellow St. John's wort flowers into a bottle outside another cabin. Down by the sauna, someone is having an evening swim.

There's an intimate feel to the evening.

When the old archipelago hands built their cabins in the outer skerries, they were not principally intent on intimacy. You built where the fishing was good, where there was shelter for boats and where there was a suitable spot for a cabin. Often, there was little flat land for building so the cabins tended to be grouped close to each other.

There are lots of settlements in the outer archipelago although many were neglected in the first half of the century. But Röder Bodskär's has been preserved as the treasure it is. All the cabins are in good shape and the island come alive in the summer.

I pick up fragments of another village conversation: two mothers are plotting how to organise a shipment of ice cream to their desperate children. One of their friends is coming out on the boat the next day, so the plan is to get that person to buy ice cream on a stop along the way, pack it in layers of newspapers for insulation and hope for the best.

Röder wakes early. The first boats are out by six, picking up nets. Others follow shortly after. There has always been good fishing near Röder and by eight, the landing stages are buzzing with fisherfolk. At that moment, a sleek wooden gig with the lustre of a prized

piece of furniture glides into the inlet. At the rudder is Gösta Söderman of Söderöra, who built the gig himself. He's a skillful boat builder but far prefers hunting and fishing.

He's a genuine archipelago hand. The other fisherfolk are proud of the flounder and whitefish they've brought in this morning but Gösta produces two salmon. He ties up and gets to work gutting and cleaning them, watched with interest by two small boys. Gösta asks them their ages and is told they're eight and ten. This sets him off:

"I was 14 the first time I came out to Röder on my own. It was really exciting. I hadn't been here for seven years, not since the old man drowned."

Gösta Söderman guts one of his salmon catches.

The demise of Gösta's father seems not to disturb the boys, nor even interest them much. They ask Gösta what sort of boat he had on that first solo trip.

"A little wooden skiff with a seven-horsepower Johnson. My mother wasn't too happy about letting me go but I had almost been born in a boat."

The kids are wide-eyed, giving Gösta all the encouragement he needs to continue with a story about the archipelago's only big game—seals. His father was a well-known seal hunter and used to bag between 30 and 40 a year in the waters off Röder.

"A seal was worth nearly a hundred crowns. He sold the meat to summer visitors on Söderöra and the skin to shoemakers. Then he boiled the blubber for oil—a seal yields about 30 litres—and sold it for two crowns a litre."

Gösta takes his nets up to the cleaning trellises, with the two kids trailing along, peppering him with questions. When did he get his first rifle? Were there fishing rods when he was small? What does seal meat taste like?

The kids don't even notice when the ice cream arrives, carefully packaged in plastic and newspaper. The kids are deep in the mysteries of repairing fishing nets.

▶ *An aerial view of the settlement on Röder Bodskär from the southwest.*

199

Cabin Fever

The sun shines in through the eastern window of the cabin, waking me at six.

My hosts are still dreaming sweet dreams in their bunks behind the checkered curtain. It is a chilly morning in late summer. I don't feel like deserting the warmth of my bed just yet, so I lie there, looking up at a ceiling stained with the soot of years of kerosene lamp lighting. A beefy spider is weaving a web in the corner right above my head, hopefully to trap the irritating mosquito buzzing around my head.

Instead, the mosquito zooms away to the books in the southern window. Nearby, there is a mirror that has seen better days; it is cracked and speckled and of little practical use—its contribution is to create beautiful reflections on the floor and ceiling.

Space is at a premium in outer skerry cabins. Every nook and cranny is put to use.

The spider clambers towards the picture frame hanging above my bed. Oil paintings are not everyday cabin decor out here but once in while, the occasional embellishment can be permitted.

In the spring of 1918, the Swedish barque *Heidi* hit a mine just beyond the outer skerries. The wreck was blown in among the islands and people went on board. They immediately began emptying the ship of everything of value: sails, line, furniture and food—the sea giveth and the sea taketh away. Wine was discovered and a keg of *Genever* schnapps. One of the local islanders found his way into the captain's cabin and took a liking to a painting. It must have been a sight—the

hoary islander leaving the sinking ship with a framed oil painting under his arm.

◄ At first sight, the cabin is stuffed: an entire household has been stored in a space smaller than a normal bedroom. But nothing here goes unused.

After an hour, I winch myself out of bed and make a fire in the fireplace. The wood is as dry as tinder and quickly catches. I creep back to bed and lie enjoying the play of flames in the fireplace. The scene could well be from the turn of the century, were it not for a few bananas on the cupboard and a little perfume bottle above the mantel.

206

It's a well-kept cabin, presumably a little more decorated than when it was built. Most outer archipelago cabins are simple and spartanly furnished. In the early days, they were the basic prerequisite for life out here. People spent spring, summer and autumn in the skerries and since their boats were uncovered, cabins were necessary, even if some chose to sleep under a sail in a boat or on shore for shorter periods.

Most cabins consist of a single room with a small threshold. The windows are seldom large: apart from nails and kitchen tiles, they were often the only part that had to be bought. Without exception, every old cabin has a large fireplace; it was the only way to provide warmth and cook.

Cabins were kept as small as possible to economise on building materials and to make them easier to heat. On the other hand, there was the desire to make them big to be able to store things. This led to the fashion of bunk beds and small, neat chairs and tables. Space is at such a premium that cabins have to be packed as efficiently as on a boat.

The fireplace is the heart of each cabin, giving warmth and light. All cooking was done in the fireplace.

Cabins were often moved. This one was in fact built on another island in the mid-19th century. When the island's inlet became too shallow because of the rising land mass, the cabin was simply dismantled and moved to this island.

Insulation was always the biggest challenge. The oldest cabins were built of horizontal planks with the cracks stuffed with moss. Floors and roofs were often insulated using anthills! Islands closer to the mainland were raided for anthills in winter when the ants were underground. The structures were composed mostly of dry pine needles, which made wonderful insulating material. The walls and roof of my own cabin, built in 1925, are filled with anthills, making it cosy even in winter.

Cabins were never locked in the old days. Everyone had the right to shelter, even if owners had precedence. Today, every single cabin is locked; the invasion of the pleasure boats has made anything else out of the question.

I awake with a jerk; I must have fallen asleep. On the pressure-gas stove in the covered threshold, a coffee pot is hissing. I observe that the mosquito has finally fallen victim to the web. From outside, my host announces breakfast, adding:

"Put on something warm. Autumn's in the air."

Built in the first half of the 19th century. In those days, they were modestly equipped and furnished.

Built in the mid-19th century. Headroom is 162 centimetres, or about five feet, four inches.

Built in the second half of the 19th century. Moved in the 1870s to its present site in the outer islands.

Built in the first half of the 19th century and moved to the outer archipelago in 1864.

Built in 1930, with extra space and room to straighten your back in.

Built in 1961, an example of the latest generation of archipelago cabins.

▲ *The fireplace in this 1925 cabin seems far too large. But the fireplace was more than a place to cook; it was a source of light and a place to dry clothes.*

▶ *It wasn't until the mid-20th century that primus stoves and gas became common. The entrance passage is often used as a kitchen. The cabin is from the first half of the 19th century.*

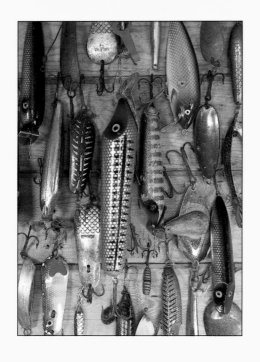

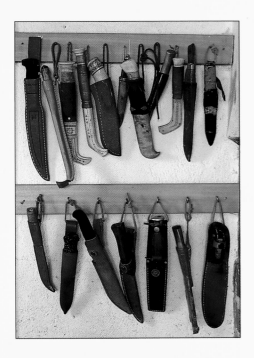

In the skerries, an outhouse is more than a sanitation facility; it's also a place for contemplation. The choice of site was important and the outhouse was often blessed with an extremely good view. Less common was interior decoration, such as in this early '60s example. A 30-year collection of driftwood and flotsam, mostly wooden spirits cases, is highlighted by cartoons and vintage pin-ups.

Glass for window panes was almost the only material the islanders needed to buy when they built their cabins in the skerries. Everything else could be found in the woods or in the sea. Often, there was only one window and its placement was carefully chosen. It was to provide light but also a view of the boat. And ideally, a panorama of the sea to give an idea of weather conditions.

215

The Collosus

Svenska Björn

There's something absurd about the structure—right in the middle of the sea, there's a ten-storey building cocking a snoot at the elements. Its 32 metres suggest a rocket, ready for launching, smack in the middle of the Baltic.

"That's no spaceship, kid,"he boasts, "It's a monument to the art of building."

His full name is Nils Ahlberg and he is a service engineer at the Swedish Shipping and Navigation Administration. For 40 years, he has been servicing the larger lighthouses. His mission has been to keep them lit. A lighthouse light must never go out.

When we unload our gear from the helicopter, Nils is a Christmas tree of bags, spare parts and tools. On the flight out, he was dressed in jacket and tie but now swiftly changes to worn work clothes, topped off with an ancient leather vest.

A living room out at sea, where Nils has spent many long evenings.

"I inherited it from my uncle,"he says, patting his chest.

We climb into the lantern section and I feel instant disappointment. Instead of a huge, rotating lamp, I see that rotation is simulated by a battery of 128 spotlights shining in different directions in a pattern. Nils disappears down the hold ladders to the guts of the lighthouse, followed by helicopter pilot Ulf Näsström, to check the generator that runs around the clock, supplying the lighthouse with electricity. I choose a slower route, investigating each storey in turn.

◄ *Not easily shifted. The lighthouse may well be standing on the seabed without additional anchorage but the building weighs a stable 15,000 tonnes.*

The top four and two lowest are filled with technical equipment; the four in between contain cabins, a sitting room, a kitchen, the lighthouse captain's office and similar spaces. Everything—furniture, light fixtures, tableware—was brought here in 1968 when the lighthouse was built to replace the old lightship. Unlike other larger lighthouses, Svenska Björn has never had a permanent crew. It was built to be almost entirely automated but was furnished because it was manned for the initial few months.

There is something spooky about exploring this huge building, abandoned to its fate out in the middle of the sea. There are books, papers and personal effects, all apparently untouched for decades. On one of the radiators, carrying

220

oil-fuelled warmth to the living spaces, there's a pair of boots that Nils left here in 1971. He claims to have a pair of boots or shoes in most lighthouses along Sweden's East coast.

"It's the easiest way," he explains, "Don't have to carry so much."

After spending a few hours with the engines, Nils adjourns to the kitchen and yells at us to come for lunch. His voice echoes throughout the lighthouse. Ulf climbs up from the lower platform where he has been pulling in vain for cod.

A final moment of light. Nils sees that two of the 128 lamps have burned out. There is no point replacing them—next week it will all be over.

They've been working together for 15 years and have spent a lot of time checking the major lighthouses of the Baltic. After all that time, they have a tendency to get slightly nostalgic and start reminiscing. There was the time a storm was blowing 65 miles an hour and they had to crawl to the helicopter to keep from being blown off the platform. And the time when fog forced them to stay on a lighthouse in the southern Baltic and their rations were used up. They ate nothing but cod for two days.

"More coffee?" asks Ulf. Nils nods and spoons in some sugar.

They don't smile much at each other but there is a sort of gentleness between them. I get a strong feeling that these are two lighthouse keepers who have shared a lifetime of experiences.

This is a journey more than touched by melancholy—this is the autumn of 1993 and it is the very last time that Nils comes out to Svenska Björn. In a week's time, it will be extinguished for good.

"There's no use for it anymore," says Nils. "It costs too much to keep going and it turns out that commercial shipping doesn't depend on the light."

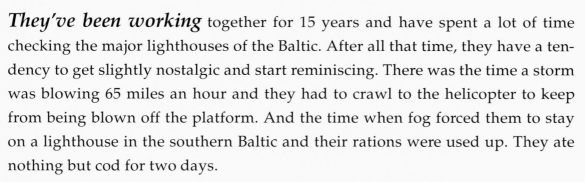

There is wounded pride in his voice. It has not been long since the lighthouse was built and was seen to be vital for safety. A week from now, staff from the Maritime Administration will arrive to turn off the machines, leaving a simple warning light to stop boats sailing right into the lighthouse.

The sun is setting and we have to fly home before it gets dark. Suddenly, we have to hurry to load the chopper and there is no longer time for regrets. But when we take off, Nils turns back one last time to the lighthouse and waves farewell. The lamp blinks back.

Lookout

Söderarm

The decorations on the wind-lashed Christmas tree compete bravely with the light from the lighthouse, built in 1839.

Christmas Eve in the seaward skerries. The outer archipelago is at its emptiest, yet Arne Ericsson surveys the sea with a practised eye. He's comfortably slouched in a chair. At regular intervals, he glances at a radar screen in front of him. Then back out at the horizon.

It feels like the bridge of a ship; in front of us, there's a huge panel of instruments, including communications radio, double radar installations and other miscellaneous gear. To the north, we can see Tjärven lighthouse and to the east, Flötjan and Lågskär blink reassuringly. The slight trembling of the building suggests a ship slicing through water. But it's the wind playing tricks—the lookout post on Söderarm island is firmly rooted to the earth.

Somebody is here, 24 hours a day, 365 days a year, looking out over the archipelago and the Sea of Åland. Their job is to foresee and prevent accidents at sea. There's a telephone line for people to ring at any time for the latest on water and wind conditions, to leave messages or even to put out a call for a missing person. I sometimes ring them myself, to leave word when I'm out in my kayak, heading for the seaward skerries. Then I know that if I don't get in touch with the guys within a certain time, they'll come looking.

A call to Söderam is my insurance.

A siren sounds, indicating it's the top of the hour. Arne looks at the wind meter, lifts a microphone and says into it:

"Söderarm reports northeasterly wind, 30 knots, with slightly limited visibility and snow flurries. Söderarm standing by on channel 16."

There's not a single boat light on the horizon and it's hard to see the point of broadcasting the news that there's a wind up.

Arne Ericsson on lookout duty.

"Sea rescue is largely a question of continuity; the prevention part is about information and maintaining a presence. That's why a continual stream of information is important. There's always someone out there—taxi boats, fishing boats, ferries or whatever."

◀ Söderarm is in a military zone and civilians are prohibited from landing. The island is full of secret installations.

The beam from the lighthouse has a funny effect as it sweeps through the darkness. The light snowfall glitters like confetti in the thin rays. The giant Finland-Sweden car ferry, the *Silja Serenade,* passes in the night and calls in a "Merry Christmas!" Ferry traffic is one of the main reasons for the Maritime Administration running the sea rescue station at Söderarm: over four million

226

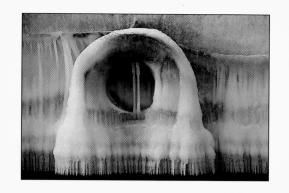

passengers a year pass within eyeshot.

By midnight, Arne's shift has stretched to six hours and he is relieved by Tom Rantala. In winter, a pool of three men are on duty for two weeks at a time (four in summer). Commuting is now commonplace but Söderarm must take the cake: lighthouse master Ivan lives on Gotland island, in the southern Baltic; Tom lives on the southern mainland and Micael Hallgren in Paris!

"I like contrasts," Micael says as he starts his shift at six o'clock on Christmas morning. He has a tin of *paté de foie gras* that he spreads on dry bread.

In the afternoon, it's Christmas dinner. Tom fixes the traditional Swedish stockfish. We have pickled herring, baked ham and all the trimmings. The only difference from a normal Christmas dinner is the ever-present crackle of the communications radio.

There is no fresh-water well on Söderarm. Water, as well as diesel fuel, is delivered every second month by the Maritime Administration's ship, Baltica.

If the Christmas holiday is calm and fine, there might well be a number of pleasure boats out in the archipelago. But the present cold snap and the wind guarantee emptiness and silence. It's so quiet that by Boxing Day, Micael is uneasy:

"Don't think it's always like this."

He hands me a binder stuffed with newspaper clippings and thank-you letters. There are lots of messages saying things like "We can never fully express our thanks for your saving us." "Thanks for your help—you're worth your weight in gold!" Or: "Angels of rescue in a canary yellow boat—THANKS for a great job. We'll remember you all our lives!"

Most moving is the story of Hans Fogdell from Sundsvall who was caught in heavy seas near Åland when the engine on his seven-metre gig seized up. He drifted helplessly for four days without being discovered. Then the duty officer at Söderarm noticed a weak blip on his radar scanner, suggesting that something might be adrift. Deciding to check, he sent two men and a rescue boat out and found the exhausted Fogdell. His thank-you was not the most loquacious of all those received but it came straight from the heart: "Thanks for my life."

The buzzer sounds and Micael grabs the microphone:

"Söderarm reports east-north-easterly, 35 knots, and good visibility. Söderarm standing by on channel 16. As always."

▶ *Winter twilight on Söderarm. Immediately to the left of the light-house is the lookout post, man-ned 24 hours a day, 365 days a year.*

The Chill

Ice build-up is a problem not only for vessels. Micael Hallgren on Söderarm island is hacking ice from a mooring chain about to snap under the weight.

Snow keeps falling but it takes some time before it settles, covering the ground on the islands.

Wind stops the dry snow from sticking to the rocks and only cracks and crevices trap the white flakes. Water temperature is just at freezing point, building stately ice sculptures on even the small stones. But the cold and the icy water indicate the danger of ice build-up, so I anchor leeward of Röder islands to hack ice from the stern.

The sky is leaden and clouds heavy with snow are piling up rapidly.

At this time of year, you can cruise for days through the outer skerries without meeting a soul. Pleasure boats have long since been hauled up onto dry land and the people who live out here seldom have occasion to come out to where the skerries give way to open sea. But I come across a taxi boat and we exchange a few observations over VHF radio. Everyone wants to talk about whether or not the water will freeze. Further north in the Baltic it freezes over every winter but the Stockholm archipelago is different. Some winters, you could drive a truck across the ice, while other years it won't freeze at all.

I continue southwest and find that ice has started to spread between the islands. My progress is blocked and I have to detour to the east. I swing by Stora Nassa before making for home at Gillöga. The days are short and at this time of year it is no fun driving a boat in the dark. The islands may be easier to see if they're covered by snow but the ice floes are almost invisible and can badly dent a propeller. In the Gillöga islands, the swell from the open sea keeps the water open, although the smallest inlets are already covered with ice. I tie up with the bow facing seawards to make it easier to break through any ice that may form during the night.

◄ *Ice is forming on the water; the little Söderarm transport boat has to swerve to avoid ice floes which could damage the propeller.*

That evening, I hear ships talking to each other on the VHF band about the ice situation further North in the Baltic. Not too far North, the northeasterlies have packed ice floes so tight that ships can pass only with the help of icebreakers. Here, the northerly keeps the water moving and stops ice from forming. As soon as the wind drops, the sea will stiffen.

234

Next morning is beautiful. The wind has veered round to the northwest and the remaining clouds could easily be mistaken for the summer variety. But the first thing that happens to me when I leave my cabin is that I fall flat on my face. Sleet must have fallen during the night, making the rocks as slippery as soap. I get up, unharmed, but mindful that you've got to make your moves carefully at this time of year.

It's time to close the cabin for the winter season; to lash the kayak to the landing stage; drag the rowing boat even further up onto land and take everything

that can freeze out of the cabin. The temperature is five degrees Celsius below zero and my fingers ache with cold when, gloveless, I untie the icy knots on the lines and cast off.

Ice settling at Hamnkobben island in the Ängskär group.

Motoring back towards the mainland, I take my time; it's a rare kind of winter day in the outer archipelago. Without ice on the water, the air tends to be so humid that blue skies are highly unusual. But today, there's a bright sun shining on the winter landscape.

Passing Grönskär island, I see movement on shore. I steer into the south inlet and tie up to icy rocks. I hear a whistle and spot the silhouette of someone carrying a log on his shoulder. Only one person I know can carry wood around that way—Erik Sundström, a man among men.

Erik salvaging a log.

"It's fine timber. It must have fallen off a ship from one of the Baltic countries. I've found four good ones so far," says Erik.

We go up to Erik's house where we share the hot chocolate and cheese sandwiches he has brought with him from the island where he lives. We listen to the weather report and learn that the coming night will be cold and still.

"Is that so?" says Erik. "There'll be ice before morning."

▶ *Winter hibernation in the settlement on Röder.*

235

An aerial view of Hamnskär island in the Kallskär group.

A bird's-eye view of the village around Byviken inlet in the Rödlöga group.

The Lilla Nassa group with Sprickopp island in the foreground.

◄ *As long as he can, Gunnar Hjertstrand tries to keep the main inlet open in the Svenska Högarna group by keeping the water in movement.*

No sculptor has been able to rival the work of Neptune and the Ice King, Boreas, when they join forces to create their art.

► The Stora Nassa group in cloud and snow. The water between skerries has iced over but the main routes are still open. But as soon as the wind dies down, they too will freeze.

241

Deep Freeze

The ice sings as we skate across the bay; there's a crunching and a swooshing sound, not unlike that of a saw bending back and forth. The ice is only a few days old and is thin and mostly smooth and shiny. Clouds are rolling in from the Baltic, still ice-free, creating dramatic reflections.

Long-distance skating is something profoundly Swedish. From November to April, there is almost unlimited scope in Eastern Sweden for this. There have been several mild winters in a row and this year's good ice is long-awaited; the word has spread like a prairie fire among Stockholm's thousands of skaters. The largest skating club has organised its usual transport from the city to the archipelago and guides to help the groups of 40 to 50 off the buses at the large jetty in the northern archipelago. There's a party atmosphere among the skaters but neither Ulf Silvander, Tomas Bergenfeldt nor I feel tempted to tag along.

"We want virgin ice," says Ulf, cutting off any discussion.

Virgin ice doesn't mean only that it is smooth and unmarked, it means that you get to out-of-the-way spots before anyone else. Virgin ice is thin.

For this reason, Ulf leads the way. He is one of the top thin-ice skaters in the country and he can skate where the ice is frighteningly thin. As he skates, he flexes his knees a little and puts his weight on one foot to feel if the ice is getting too thin. He hardly ever uses the ice-stick that every skater carries—it takes too long to stop and hack at the ice. Instead, he checks by stamping his foot and listening.

When the ice is smooth and you have the wind at your back, you can develop real pace—speeds of 20 miles an hour are not uncommon. Few experiences will give you such an intoxicating sense of freedom as zooming across smooth, virgin ice.

A thin strip of good ice. Open water to one side and broken ice to the other. One false stride and you're either wet or black and blue.

Ulf Silvander, on the trail of smooth ice.

◄ *Homeward bound from Lygna. With the wind at your back, the speed can be intoxicating.*

248

We're aiming for the Rödlöga islands but after half an hour we run into a patch of snow-covered ice clutter which presents difficulties. Once through it, we find open water.

"It's only local," says Ulf. "We'll head north."

There's a thin strip of smooth ice between the clutter and the water and we travel it at half speed. Trip and tumble to one side and you'd get hurt; to the other, you'd get a soaking.

Tomas has not had his breakfast porridge and is getting irritable. We stop and eat an early lunch: cheese sandwiches and hot chocolate in the lee of an iced-over point.

Clouds thicken and we continue eastwards. A rift forces us to take off our skates and detour over a large point. We continue on towards Norrpada via several small islands. The ice is thin and there are rifts and patches of open water. I keep 50 metres behind Ulf and see how his weight makes a depression in the ice around him. Where the ice is extra-thin, he adopts a wide-legged stance; we all try to spread our weight as much as possible. The ice sings and creaks. We feel decidedly small out on these vast expanses of water.

High islands are lookout points. Is there ice further out or open water?

Once at Norrpada, we clamber up onto one of the highest islands to survey the surrounding ice. There is open water to the east; to the south and north there are patches of open water. We glide around among islands before setting course for Rödlöga.

Suddenly, the ice gives way under Ulf and he instinctively throws himself to one side. He gets his left foot a little wet but manages to stay out of the drink. Once on his feet, he pokes a little with his ice-stick before setting off again, a little more to the right. He seems utterly unaffected.

"I'd never be skating here if Ulf wasn't along," says Tomas.

It is almost dark by the time we get to Rödlöga. We've covered fifty kilometres and my feet are aching slightly. Tomas and Ulf seem totally untouched by fatigue—their record is more than 200 kilometres in a day.

We have arranged to borrow a cabin, which is in deep freeze. It's seven Celsius below. We light a fire and Tomas begins dinner. Ulf pulls out a cellular phone and rings the answerphone at the skating club. He listens to the taped message and his eyes are gleaming as he disconnects.

"They say there's ice all the way out to the outermost skerries but that it's too thin for skating. That's where we'll head tomorrow."

Smooth ice on sea-water—there is no grander feeling of freedom!

Top-class skaters on their way to Svenska Högarna. To get around the patches of open water, they sometimes have to cross dry land.

A week earlier, we had come by boat to Fredlarna; now we're arriving on skates.

▶ *At Ängskär, a group makes the most of the last smooth ice. Heavy snow has been predicted for the following day, making the ice untraversable.*

251

Contents

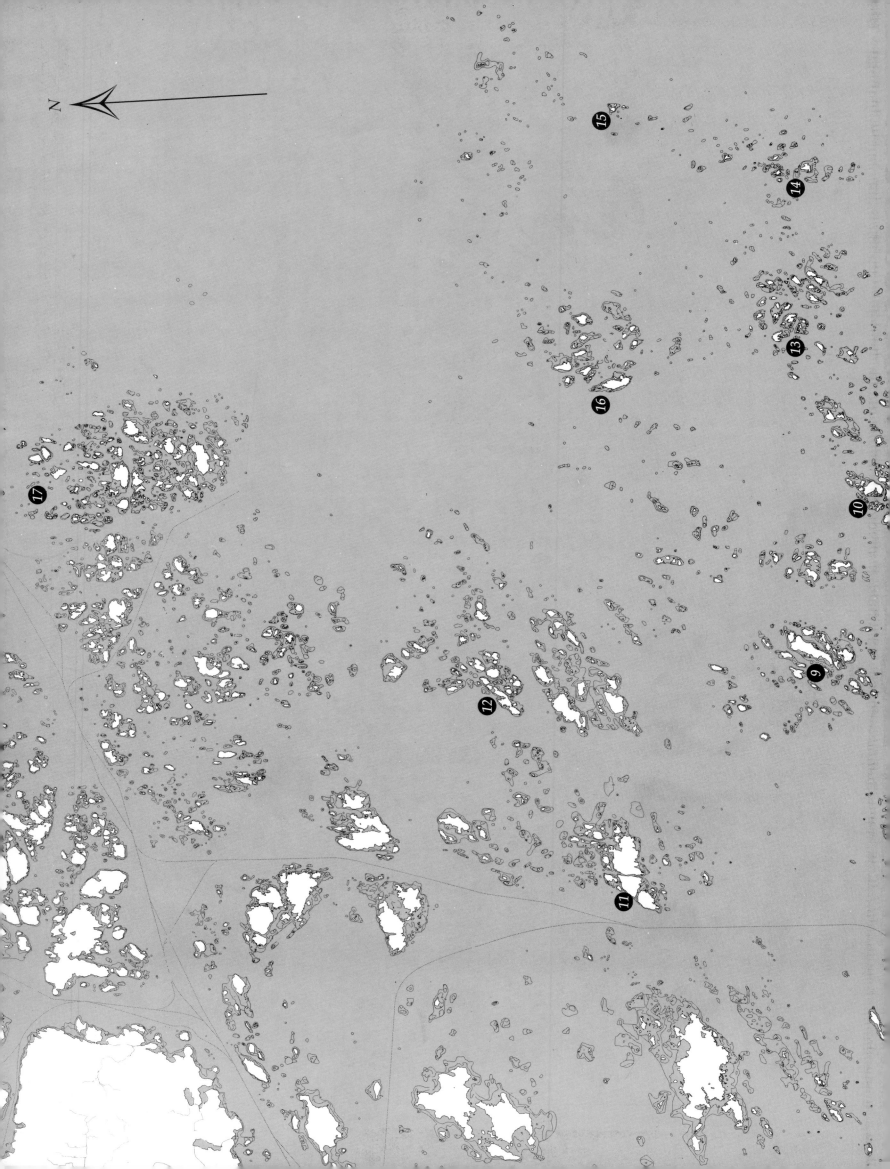